JENNIE BUTCHART

JENNIE

HERITAGE

Trailblazing Canadians

BUTCHART

GARDENER OF DREAMS

WRITTEN BY
HALEY HEALEY

ILLUSTRATED BY
KIMIKO FRASER

Heritage House Publishing Company Ltd.
heritagehouse.ca

Cataloguing information available from Library and Archives Canada
978-1-77203-481-3 (hardcover)
978-1-77203-482-0 (paperback)
978-1-77203-483-7 (ebook)

Illustrated by Kimiko Fraser
Cover and interior book design by Setareh Ashrafologhalai
Illustrations inspired by original images, courtesy of: City of Vancouver
Archives (CVA 1184-2804, CVA 1477-4, 2009-005.481, CVA 1477-1375,
CVA 289-003.381, CVA 1477-263.36, CVA 586-16705, CVA 1477-324,
CVA 586-16702); City of Victoria Archives (M00805, M06742, M10440,
M05829, M05819, M05820, M05821, M07113, M05822, M07330, M00449,
M00552, M00906, M00759); Royal BC Museum (Image J-01269);
and Esquimalt Municipal Archives (PR053-v986-018-020).

The interior of this book was produced on FSC®-certified, acid-free paper,
processed chlorine free, and printed with vegetable-based inks.

Heritage House gratefully acknowledges that the land on which we live
and work is within the traditional territories of the Lkwungen (Esquimalt
and Songhees), Malahat, Pacheedaht, Scia'new, T'Sou-ke, and
W̱SÁNEĆ (Pauquachin, Tsartlip, Tsawout, Tseycum) Peoples.

We acknowledge the financial support of the Government of Canada
through the Canada Book Fund (CBF) and the Canada Council for the
Arts, and the Province of British Columbia through the British
Columbia Arts Council and the Book Publishing Tax Credit.

28 27 26 25 24   1 2 3 4 5

Printed in China

NOTE OF TRUTH AND RECONCILIATION

This book was written on the traditional territory of the Snuneymuxw First Nation. Some of the story takes place on the traditional territory of the W̱SÁNEĆ First Nations. The author fully and completely supports truth and reconciliation and recognizes her own role in truth and reconciliation.

JENNIE was born and raised in Ontario, Canada. She lost both her parents when she was young, and grew up with her aunt and seven cousins in Owen Sound. Young Jennie was full of energy and loved trying new activities. She liked ice skating and horseback riding. She even learned to drive a carriage pulled by four horses.

When she grew up, Jennie married a man named Robert. They had two daughters and moved across Canada to Vancouver Island, British Columbia.

The couple owned a cement plant, where Jennie worked as a chemist. The cement was made of limestone from a deep hole in the ground, called a quarry. Sacks of cement from their plant were delivered all over the world by ship.

But a few years after they started this business, the quarry ran out of limestone. All that was left was a big hole filled with rusty equipment and empty rock walls.

Jennie wasn't happy. One day, she said to Robert, "Let's plant it with flowers and make it beautiful."

Once she got the idea for her garden, Jennie couldn't wait to get started. There was just one problem: she didn't know much about gardening! So, she read books about gardening and talked to people who knew a lot about plants, called botanists. She learned all she could about making things grow.

Jennie ordered soil, which was brought in by horse and buggy. She hired a landscape architect named Isaburo Kishida, who designed the garden, and workers from the cement plant to help plant it.

Jennie planted many flowers herself, some from seed. She started with roses and sweet peas. Then she planted violets, marigolds, pansies, and petunias.

To plant ivy on the tall walls of the Sunken Garden, Jennie hung high in the air in a harness called a bosun's chair.

Over the years, she added more
and more flowers to her garden.
Some seeds were gifts from friends.

Others she collected on her travels
around the world. Poppies from Asia
were bright blue with yellow centres.

Soon, Jennie's garden was
overflowing with blooms,
divided into different sections.

There was the Sunken Garden,

the Japanese Garden,

the Italian Garden,

the Mediterranean Garden,

and the Rose Garden.

Robert brought ducks, peacocks, and pigeons to live in the gardens. Fountains and structures sat between the flowers and trees.

Visitors from all over the world came to see Jennie's garden. Everyone was welcome—locals, tourists, and even royalty!

Through good times and bad,
the gardens always stayed open.

During World War II, there were barely enough workers to keep it running. But Jennie was determined not to shut it down.

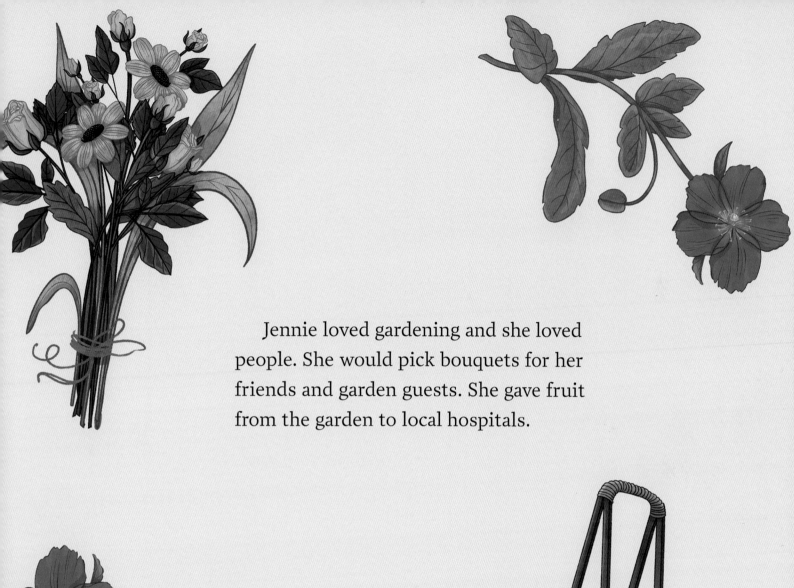

Jennie loved gardening and she loved people. She would pick bouquets for her friends and garden guests. She gave fruit from the garden to local hospitals.

After many years, when Jennie was too old to keep running the gardens, her grandson took over. He kept the tearoom open and brought in puppet shows, musical symphonies, and even fireworks.

The Butchart Gardens
is a special place. It is so
special that it's called a
National Historic Site of
Canada. Millions of people
visit each year and enjoy
the garden Jennie created.

HISTORICAL TIMELINE

1866
Jennie is born in Toronto, Ontario.

1902–8
Jennie and her husband, Robert, move to Vancouver Island. They build a cement plant on a limestone deposit in Tod Inlet, near Victoria. For a few years, their successful business supplies many construction projects up and down the west coast of North America.

By 1908, the Butcharts' quarry runs out of limestone, leaving a giant pit in their backyard.

1911–25
The Butcharts' house is remodelled and expanded by renowned Canadian architect Samuel Maclure, who was famous in the Arts and Crafts movement.

1921–29
The gardens, which began as an idea in Jennie's mind a decade earlier, are completed, expanded, and opened to the public. Everyone is welcome to explore, marvel, and even pick flowers, free of charge, seven days a week.

1939–45
During the Second World War, with many Canadians are serving overseas, the gardens suffer from lack of staff. However, they stay open throughout the War and beyond.

As she gets older, Jennie takes a step back from the business of running the gardens. She and Robert gift the gardens their grandson.

1950
Jennie Butchart dies, but her legacy lives on.

2004
The Butchart Gardens are designated a National Historic Site of Canada.

Two totem poles—carved by Master Carvers Charles Elliott of the Tsartlip Nation and Doug La Fortune of the Tsawout Nation—are raised in recognition of the original inhabitants of the land on which The Butchart Gardens were built.

TODAY
The Butchart Gardens are still owned by the Butchart family and visited by over a million people per year.

HALEY HEALEY is a high school counsellor, registered clinical counsellor, and the bestselling author of books for all ages about extraordinary historical women. Her books include the Trailblazing Canadians series; *Her Courage Rises* (a finalist for the 2023 Sheila A. Egoff Children's Literature Prize); *On Their Own Terms: True Stories of Trailblazing Women of Vancouver Island*; and *Flourishing and Free: More Stories of Trailblazing Women of Vancouver Island*. A self-proclaimed trailblazing woman herself, she enjoys exploring Vancouver Island's trails, waters, and wilderness. She has an avid interest in wild places and lives in Nanaimo, British Columbia.

J. KING YORK

KIMIKO FRASER is an illustrator and historian-in-training. She grew up constantly making—drawing, painting, knitting, sculpting, bookbinding, etc.—and has never learned how to stop. She is the illustrator of the Trailblazing Canadians series and *Her Courage Rises: 50 Trailblazing Women of British Columbia and the Yukon*. She holds a bachelor of arts (honours History, major Visual Arts) from the University of Victoria. She works with many mediums to create her illustrations, including watercolour, digital, ink, and tea. Most of her work is inspired by her interest in plants, history, and folktales. She lives in Victoria, British Columbia.